Marriage

Anna & Nick Brooker

...for those times when we want to hear God's word speaking to us clearly

Marriage

Anna & Nick Brooker

Published by
The Bible Reading Fellowship
First Floor, Elsfield Hall
15–17 Elsfield Way, Oxford OX2 8FG

ISBN 1 84101 427 3
First published 2005
10 9 8 7 6 5 4 3 2 1 0

Acknowledgments
Unless otherwise indicated, scripture quotations are taken from the Contemporary
English Version, copyright © American Bible Society 1991, 1992, 1995. Used by
permission. Anglicizations © British and Foreign Bible Society 1997.

Scripture quotations taken from the Holy Bible, New International Version,
copyright © 1973, 1978, 1984 by International Bible Society, are used by
permission of Hodder & Stoughton Limited. All rights reserved. 'NIV' is a
registered trademark of International Bible Society. UK trademark number
1448790.

Scripture quotations taken from The New Revised Standard Version of the Bible,
Anglicized Edition, copyright © 1989, 1995 by the Division of Christian
Education of the National Council of the Churches of Christ in the United States
of America, are used by permission. All rights reserved.

Scripture quotations taken from the New Living Version, published by Tyndale
Charitable Trust, are used by permission of Tyndale House Publishers.

Common Worship: Pastoral Services copyright © The Archbishops' Council 2000.

A catalogue record for this book is available from the British Library

Printed by Gutenberg Press, Tarxien, Malta

Introduction

Recently we went to a wedding. It was a true celebration of God's love for the couple, their families, friends and colleagues. The bride and groom were so joyful that they managed to smile throughout the photographs and well beyond. The guests caught their infectious delight. It was a taste of heaven, a day to remember. That couple get a mention in these notes for the original way in which one proposed to the other—you'll have to read on to find out how!

Marriage, despite the gloomy statistics, is still popular. And those who marry in church recognize that marriage is a gift of God to humanity, his best plan for how a man and a woman can live together within a secure and loving commitment. We hope that these readings will demonstrate loud and clear that God is fully committed to those who choose to marry, and offers us his love and resources for the journey we undertake with our partner.

So much of the Bible is about human relationships that we were spoilt for choice in selecting these passages. Despite cultural differences across the centuries, we recognize in biblical characters human tendencies and characteristics that are universal. A look at three Bible marriages and what we can learn from them seemed like a good place to start.

Naturally, each of us is heavily influenced by the marriages of others: primarily our parents and other family members, and our friends. What we see in these marriages determines our expectations of marriage, and it is important to recognize this and discuss it with each other. In our case, for example, one of our mothers married someone six years younger than herself, the other someone 17 years older. And where one of us was the oldest, born within a year of the parents' wedding, the other was the youngest, born nearly ten years into their marriage.

In the marriages of Adam and Eve, and Isaac and Rebekah, the difficulties are plain to see, as communication and trust break down. Sadly, we learn much from others' experiences of marital problems and breakdown, although we can never fully understand, much less apportion blame. In the case of Mary and Joseph, however, we have a model of a couple whose mutual trust and faith in God equipped them for challenges and responsibilities of eternal significance. Good marriages have tremendous potential to bring love, compassion and hope not only to the couple themselves but, through them, to many others.

This concept of marriage 'for the common good' is highlighted in the *Common Worship* Marriage Service, which we have used as the theme for the second week's readings. The big day is such a focus of attention and energy that the bouquets and photographs can begin to take priority over vows and prayer.

We hope that taking time to reflect on the words and the biblical passages behind the vows will enrich your appreciation of the promises you made, or are about to make. Standing before our chosen partner, in public and yet in total honesty and intimacy, has to be one of the holiest experiences we will ever know on earth. It is good to return to it together, to reinvigorate our relationship as we remember the firm foundations that were laid as we made our vows to each other in the sight of God.

So much attention is paid in popular culture to the trappings of the wedding ceremony, the parties, presents, drinks and dresses, that there is little time to consider the deeper values and key priorities which are vital to marriage. Rather like the ill-assorted couples on *Blind Date*, what we all seek is a partner who is considerate, kind, respectful and trustworthy, and this soon matters far more than their dress sense or taste in music. The virtue of loyalty is emphasized repeatedly in our notes, probably because it is there repeatedly in the Bible, but also because it is so fundamental to the growth of love and trust over the years.

Abraham Lincoln is reputed to have said of marriage, 'It is not best to swap horses while crossing the river!' While choice and novelty are hallowed values in a consumerist age, the wonder of growing old together cannot be overlooked. The fruit of a mature marriage is companionship, friendship, contentment and unity. Such marriages enrich the lives of whole families and communities as they take their course through joys, sorrows and everyday routine. We hope that these readings will enable you together to draw on God's resources for your relationship and to be excited and encouraged by the promises of his love and faithfulness.

Unless otherwise stated, quotations are from the Contemporary English Version of the Bible.

GENESIS 2:18, 22b–23a, 24

Adam and Eve (part 1)

*The Lord God said, 'It isn't good for the man to live alone.
I need to make a suitable partner for him.' … The Lord God
brought her to the man, and the man exclaimed. 'Here is
someone like me! She is part of my body, my own flesh and
bones…' That's why a man will leave his own father and
mother. He marries a woman, and the two of them become
like one person.*

All of God's creation is good, with one exception: it is not good for
the man to live alone. As human beings, we all need relationship,
and marriage answers that deep need. The sense of recognition that
Adam experiences when he meets Eve is an essential part of falling
in love, of discovering that the other person has become an integral
part of our hopes and dreams for the future. When these feelings
lead to action and commitment, a new bond is established.

The marriage relationship, as deep as that between parent and
child, must take priority over pre-existing relationships in order
to succeed. Hackneyed mother-in-law jokes have a point: unless
'apron strings' are cut, there will be conflicting priorities for the
couple. It takes time and space to establish a relationship in-
dependent of parents, friends, former partners, even children.
Hard as it is to achieve, this prioritizing is the best way to ensure
that other commitments do not get in the way of the marriage.

The public ceremony of marriage is both a celebration of the
union of two people and a declaration of intent. Within that legal
certainty, and with the cooperation of friends and family, partners
work to make the union a practical reality. Paradoxically, it is both
an immediate change and a lifelong process.

*'Love is altogether a much deeper, give-and-take, affectionate relationship
than being "in" love.' (Frank Muir, writing about his marriage)*

GENESIS 3:6–8 (ABRIDGED)

Adam and Eve (part 2)

*The woman stared at the fruit. It looked beautiful and tasty.
She wanted the wisdom that it would give her, and she ate
some of the fruit. Her husband was there with her, so she
gave some to him, and he ate it too. Straight away… they
realized they were naked… Late in the afternoon… the man
and woman heard the Lord God walking in the garden. They
were frightened and hid behind some trees.*

Eve eats the apple; Adam doesn't stop her; both share the blame.
Neither of them really trusts God's warning that the beautiful fruit
on that particular tree will bring death, not life. Had Eve admitted
what she was thinking to Adam, perhaps together they could have
reached a less disastrous decision—who knows?

Our human tendency to say 'It's not my fault' always has serious
consequences, and in the closeness of marriage the choice between
honesty and deception is a stark one. It is always easier to excuse
our lateness, lack of consideration or forgetfulness, or the scratch
on the car, by blaming someone else. Why? Maybe we fear our
partner's reaction, or we're too proud to admit our own faults. But
as we see graphically with Adam and Eve, whereas the truth sets us
free, deception changes us from being relaxed and open with each
other and God, to hiding from him and each other.

Our honesty, however, can open up the opportunity for our
partner to reassure and support us. Let's not be fooled that hiding
the truth will 'protect' our partner from hurt. Whatever the
difficulty, an honest response to it will strengthen our marriage.

*'It is only inasmuch as you see someone else as he or she really is here
and now, and not as they are in your memory or your desire or your
imagination or projection, that you can truly love them.' (Anthony de
Mello)*

GENESIS 24:12a, 15a

Isaac and Rebekah (part 1)

'You, Lord, are the God my master Abraham worships. Please keep your promise to him and let me find a wife for Isaac today…' While he was still praying, a beautiful unmarried young woman came by with a water jar on her shoulder.

Abraham's most trusted servant has been sent on a mission—to find the perfect wife for Isaac. The romantic 'coincidence' of Rebekah's appearance just as he is praying is worthy of the silver screen. But then so is every account of how a couple met and fell in love, how the story of their relationship began. Few people can remain unmoved by such accounts of lives transformed, and personal and family histories made.

'How we met' is a good story to tell, again and again: it helps keep hold of the uniqueness of our relationship, especially at stages when mundane routines and responsibilities seem to dominate. The memories we share become part of the 'story' of our marriage, a shared yet private treasure. As the story continues, pausing to look back helps us to see how far we have come, and to have a clearer sense of where we are going.

There will be times when we face more change than stability, through births or bereavements, sudden crises or increasing pressures. Such experiences can be woven into the ongoing story of our marriage, through listening, talking and praying together and with others close to us. As with every good story, there are quiet bits and exciting bits, everyday events and daring exploits, adventures and homecomings. The cast of characters grows and changes, and the setting is the home in which we live.

'Home is where life makes up its mind. It is there—with fellow family members—we hammer out our convictions on the anvil of relationships.' (Charles Swindoll)

GENESIS 24:63–65, 67 (ABRIDGED)

Isaac and Rebekah (part 2)

One evening [Isaac]… saw a group of people approaching on camels. So he started towards them. Rebekah… got down from her camel, and asked, 'Who is that man?' 'He is my master Isaac,' the servant answered. Then Rebekah covered her face with her veil… Isaac took Rebekah into the tent where his mother had lived… and Rebekah became his wife. He loved her and was comforted over the loss of his mother.

Happily ever after? The fairytale ending is just the beginning for Isaac and Rebekah, as they finally meet and fall in love. You can read about Isaac and Rebekah's long and tempestuous relationship in Genesis 25—35. After 20 years of infertility, the longed-for baby turns out to be troublesome twins. Later, famine forces them to uproot and live among enemies and foreigners, with whom their son Esau intermarries, to their great distress. Deception and estrangement follow, but by God's grace reconciliation and healing are also possible. The cycle of deception, infertility, sibling rivalry and estrangement continues into Jacob's family, again redeemed through human and divine forgiveness.

From the outset it is clear that Rebekah is not simply marrying Isaac, but entering into a complicated family. Even if we choose to elope to a desert island, our marriage will still have far-reaching implications in family terms. Rebekah doesn't have a mother-in-law to relate to, but lives with the memory of a beloved wife and mother whom she never knew. She comforts her husband in his grief, as well as taking on the matriarchal role in the family, later made all the more difficult by her childlessness (Genesis 25:21).

What roles are you expected to play in the wider families that you joined or are about to join on marriage? How can you support each other in coping with this?

LUKE 1:26–28, 30–32, 38 (ABRIDGED)

Mary

God sent the angel Gabriel… with a message for a virgin named Mary. She was engaged to Joseph from the family of King David. The angel greeted Mary and said, 'You are truly blessed! … God is pleased with you, and you will have a son. His name will be Jesus. He will be great and will be called the Son of God Most High…' Mary said, 'I am the Lord's servant! Let it happen as you have said.'

How many times have you heard these words read in a carol service? We can become so used to the extraordinary events that heralded Jesus' birth that we overlook the real human beings involved. Mary could never have anticipated what God had in store when she agreed to marry the local carpenter. Now at a stroke, her wedding plans are shattered.

Whether you are preparing to marry, like Mary, or are already married, you will have many hopes and dreams invested in your relationship. Do you share them with each other? Do you give time both to speak and listen? I suspect that Mary and Joseph had talked and listened to one another enough for trust to begin to grow between them, rooted in their faith in God and in his good plans for their lives.

Mary's reply to the angel is remarkably calm and confident. Yes, she asks questions (vv. 29, 34), but it becomes clear that she has her priorities worked out. *Her* plans may be in ruins, but she says a resounding 'Yes' to God's plans for her marriage and family. Each of us will face times when we feel called to put our own plans on hold and submit to the needs of others. The stronger our trust in God and in each other, the better we can face such times together.

'Trust is one of the fundamental aspects of life… Only trust allows the soul room to breathe.' (Wolfhart Pannenberg)

MATTHEW 1:19–20, 24

Joseph

Joseph was a good man and did not want to embarrass Mary in front of everyone. So he decided to call off the wedding quietly. While Joseph was thinking about this, an angel from the Lord came to him in a dream. The angel said, 'Joseph, the baby that Mary will have is from the Holy Spirit. Go ahead and marry her…' After Joseph woke up, he and Mary were soon married, just as the Lord's angel had told him to do.

Given the unfortunate situation, Joseph could have 'divorced' Mary publicly. His reputation would have remained untainted, his family's honour satisfied. Instead, he decides on a quiet parting, to protect Mary as much as possible. We can only imagine his pain and disappointment at giving up the young woman he loved.

Yet the angel's proposals allow him to follow his heart. He will take care of Mary and Jesus, whom he will bring up as his own son, part of the line of David, from whom he is descended. Later, he and Mary will have a family of their own. So often we think that God will ask us to give things up or go in the opposite direction to our feelings, but Joseph is asked to take on responsibility for what is dearest to him. It will involve many challenges, but Joseph is just the person to support Mary and Jesus, and he is eager to do so.

Whenever two people marry, particularly if they have been married before or have children already, the responsibilities involved may seem daunting. What we can know is the guidance of God as we pray and talk through decisions. He will bless us with the ability to understand each other's needs and anxieties, and will equip us with wisdom, patience and energy. God wants marriages and families to work, and he helps us as we try to ensure they do.

'Never be afraid to trust an unknown future to a known God.' (Corrie ten Boom)

1 JOHN 4:7b–8, 12, 19

To have and to hold

*Love comes from God, and when we love each other, it shows
that we have been given new life. We are now God's children,
and we know him. God is love, and anyone who doesn't love
others has never known him... No one has ever seen God.
But if we love each other, God lives in us, and his love is truly
in our hearts... We love because God loved us first.*

Love is a sign of new life, like the first snowdrops of spring. We all
know people who have 'come alive' when they met their partner,
blossoming as individuals and couples within a loving relationship. It is less easy to recognize how we ourselves change through
the love we experience.

John emphasizes that love is given, not manufactured from our
own resources. We can be certain that God wants us to love each
other, and to build strong marriages, so we can ask for the gift
of love on a daily basis. Love will then provide the energy and
motivation to wash up or do the shopping *again*, to bite back the
words of unhelpful criticism, to forgive and let go of hurt. Just the
other day Anna left some important papers by the front door as she
left for work. She phoned home, and immediately Nick offered to
drive them over, in time for the meeting when Anna needed them.
It was love in action, and it made all the difference to her.

In the church marriage service, each partner 'takes' the other
to be their husband or wife, 'to have and to hold from this day
forward...' What does this taking, having and holding mean in
practice? It is active, not passive; it is constant, not dependent on
other circumstances, and it is ongoing, rather than static.

*'Marriage... is given that as man and woman grow together in love and
trust, they may be united with one another in heart, body and mind.'*
(Common Worship *Marriage Service*)

GALATIANS 5:16, 19, 22–23a, 26 (CEV)

For better, for worse

If you are guided by the Spirit, you won't obey your selfish desires… People's desires make them give in to immoral ways, filthy thoughts, and shameful deeds… God's Spirit makes us loving, happy, peaceful, patient, kind, good, faithful, gentle and self-controlled… But don't be conceited or make others jealous by claiming to be better than they are.

A young man recently proposed to his girlfriend as they made a bungee jump together. Her 'Yeeesss!' echoed up and down the ravine. On their wedding day they 'took the plunge' again together. It is electrifyingly exciting and stupendously scary, and it lasts far longer than a bungee jump. Part of the risk of marriage is that we don't know what the future holds.

Scientists are now working on tests to predict the genetic likelihood of contracting terminal illnesses. Such information could be used to prevent people being offered life assurance, or equally to enable money to be made fraudulently out of tragic circumstances. The impact on marriage would be devastating. Our commitment to each other has to be unconditional and it will never be possible to protect ourselves from circumstances such as accidents, illness and bereavement.

It is possible, however, to ensure that we are inwardly prepared for the inevitable crises that are part of life and marriage. The Holy Spirit will guide us in very practical and positive ways. The list of qualities or 'fruit' of the Spirit in this passage provide a checklist of all we need. Note the final warning, though: such fulfilled living is given by God through his Spirit, not the result of any superiority on our part, and our response must be gratitude, not pride.

'May their marriage be life-giving and life-long, enriched by your presence and strengthened by your grace.' (Common Worship Marriage Service)

PHILIPPIANS 4:4, 6–7

For richer, for poorer

*Always be glad because of the Lord! I will say it again:
be glad… Don't worry about anything, but pray about
everything. With thankful hearts offer up your prayers
and requests to God. Then, because you belong to
Christ Jesus, God will bless you with peace that
no one can completely understand. And this peace
will control the way you think and feel.*

Nick tells friends that he married for a car! Since it was an ancient banger, with a top speed of 50 mph, Anna is comforted to think that there must have been other reasons. Yet in these days of pervasive consumerism, it's easy for money or possessions to be our main concern, even if we don't follow the celebrity fashion for prenuptial financial agreements.

The harsh reality, however, is that finance is the rock against which many marriages stumble. It needs to be discussed honestly, planned carefully, reviewed frequently and agreed mutually. This will help us to withstand pressures such as redundancy, illness, housing costs and inflation.

How *can* Paul say, 'Don't worry about anything'? The answer comes immediately: be thankful. Appreciation of what we have is the surest way to stop worrying about what we don't have. It also redirects us to recognize God's generosity, and dispels the dissatisfaction that leads us to want more than we really need. God's peace flows into our lives as we choose to be thankful in all circumstances, and to turn our anxieties into prayers. Amazing, but it works!

Discuss, plan, review and agree: take time together to apply this process to an area of your life about which you are anxious. Then, 'with thankful hearts, offer up your prayers and requests to God'.

ROMANS 8:31b, 38–39

In sickness and in health

*If God is on our side, can anyone be against us? …
I am sure that nothing can separate us from God's love—
not life or death, not angels or spirits, not the present or
the future, and not powers above or powers below. Nothing
in all creation can separate us from God's love for us
in Christ Jesus our Lord!*

'Rangers till I die,' sang the fans, even as their team failed yet again to win promotion to the next division of the football league. It almost became the anthem of defeat, but it also marked out the fair-weather fans from the real diehards. Loyalty to a sporting team, or to friends or children, is sadly more common, perhaps even more acceptable, in our society than loyalty to one's wife or husband. Yet loyalty—obstinate, unmovable, deliberately chosen—is a mark of true love.

If we are looking for a model of loyalty, here it is. The 'love which never lets me go' of the old hymn is the anchor to hold us as storms and waves crash in. Our pattern for loyalty and faithfulness is the love of God, love as strong as death itself. And here too is the resource to draw on at the times when it is hardest to keep on loving each other.

Paul makes incredible claims about God's love. It is stronger than all we most fear, including the losses that separate us from those we love. God's love is for us; even if we are separated from each other, we will never be separated from God's love.

'Eternal God, Creator and redeemer, from whom comes every good and perfect gift… breathe into their marriage the strength of your holy and life-giving Spirit. Send upon them the gift of love that puts no limit on its faith or forbearance.' (Common Worship *Marriage Service*)

1 CORINTHIANS 13:4–8

To love and to cherish

Love is kind and patient, never jealous, boastful, proud, or rude. Love isn't selfish or quick-tempered. It doesn't keep a record of wrongs that others do. Love rejoices in the truth, but not in evil. Love is always supportive, loyal, hopeful, and trusting. Love never fails!

What does the word 'cherish' make you think of? Your answer will probably reveal something about how you prefer to express and receive love. For Anna, it evokes memories of her favourite aunt and uncle, married for over 40 years. They always seemed happiest sitting together in front of the fire, chatting, laughing or doing the crossword. She basked in the warmth of their relationship and loved to visit them, as did many friends and neighbours.

A friend, married less than a year and newly pregnant, is also about to move house and start a new job. 'In the past, in fact all my life,' she told us, 'transitions like this have been really difficult and terrifying. But with Dave alongside me, I know it will be different this time.'

In *The Marriage Course* (Alpha, 2000), Nicky and Sila Lee talk about the five 'expressions of love': loving words, kind actions, quality time, thoughtful presents and physical affection. The relative importance of these will vary from person to person, and it is good to learn which of the five is most important to our partner, and to practise it regularly. As Lucy, of Charles M. Schulz's *Peanuts* cartoon, observes, 'All I really need is love, but a little chocolate now and then doesn't hurt!' Take time to talk together about what makes you each feel cherished by the other.

'To have and to hold from this day forward; for better for worse, for richer for poorer, in sickness and in health, to love and to cherish, till death us do part.' (Common Worship *Marriage Service*)

1 PETER 1:3, 5, 7a

Till death us do part

Praise God, the Father of our Lord Jesus Christ. God is so good, and by raising Jesus from death, he has given us new life and a hope that lives on… You have faith in God, whose power will protect you until the last day. Then he will save you, just as he has always planned to do… Your faith will be like gold that has been tested in a fire.

The average career for someone now starting work will encompass 19 different jobs. Archbishop Rowan Williams recently expressed his fear that in an age when the 'portfolio' approach is applied to careers, it is also applied to personal relationships. The pursuit of short-term goals and experiences leaves little space for lasting satisfaction or maturity.

Marriage, like Christianity, is a long-term commitment, focusing not on instant success but hope for the future. As our relationship is tested, it will be strengthened and purified, becoming like precious, indestructible gold. Making this long-term commitment is indeed an act of faith. Yet when our faith is in God, whose plans for our lives are long-term and hope-filled, we can be confident.

At times, however, we all still need to know the answer to the Beatles' famous question: 'Will you still need me, will you still feed me, when I'm sixty-four?' Twenty years into marriage we lived apart midweek, while Anna trained for ministry. Returning home each weekend, she needed to know that she was still needed, not just as mother but as wife too. The details became important: flowers awaiting her arrival, prioritizing evenings together over time with friends, and the midweek phone calls to start and end each day, whether we felt like talking or not.

'Let peace spring from their faithfulness to each other and flow deeper with the passing years.' (Common Worship *Marriage Service*)

JAMES 1:19, 26

Listening

My dear friends, you should be quick to listen and slow to speak or to get angry… If you think you are being religious, but can't control your tongue, you are fooling yourself, and everything you do is useless.

It is wise to think before we speak, and nowhere more so than in our marriages. As words cause hurt and pain, so also they can promote healing and assurance, affirming friendship and love. Each of us is deeply affected by the words spoken to us by our husband or wife: the potential for good or harm is tremendous. Do we find this an awesome responsibility or an exciting challenge?

Listening takes time. So often, we interrupt each other, assuming we know what our partner is about to say. Listening is vital to appreciate what they are really thinking and feeling. Otherwise, frustration and resentment ensue, and small misunderstandings soon grow into great divides. Ultimately, we stop talking to each other about anything more significant than the routine necessities of everyday life.

When are good times for you to talk and listen to each other? We often do so while walking the dog, sitting in the garden or even going out for a coffee, away from phone calls and other distractions. Just half an hour can make a huge difference in a busy week.

Samuel Taylor Colderidge once said, 'The most happy marriage I can picture or imagine to myself would be the union of a deaf man to a blind woman.' As we work together to build strong marriages, let us ask God for 'the hearing ear and the seeing eye' (Proverbs 20:12, NLV) with which to support and encourage each other.

'There are times when what we need most are not words of advice or direction, but the knowledge that someone is there, accepting us as we are, that we are not, after all, alone.' (Anne Long)

PROVERBS 27:17, 19 (NRSV)

Self-awareness

Iron sharpens iron, and one person sharpens the wits of another… Just as water reflects the face, so one human heart reflects another.

Marriage is a great way to find out what we're really like. As we get to know each other better, so our own strengths and weaknesses are brought into sharper focus. It's uncomfortable at times, but also a source of growth and development for each person.

God wants to enrich us as individuals through our partners. Sometimes this is obvious, because our personalities, skills and experiences complement each other. Sometimes it is less clear, but we realize how we are growing through the influence that our husband or wife has on us. One partner may be methodical in preparations for an event, while the other may get ready in time, but only just. Such differences cause frustration and arguments. Conversely, they can be a mirror on to our own habits and character, which God gives us to reflect our need for personal development.

Only after many years of stress on both sides did we realize how best to manage Christmas: Nick plans and cooks the meals, Anna decorates the house and table, and we're both happy. Inherited roles within marriage may become a straitjacket, so we need to agree what works for us now, which is unlikely to be the same as it was for our parents or others whose marriages we have observed.

By looking positively at our differences and strengths, we sharpen self-awareness and understanding of each other. Without this, we may echo Professor Higgins in *My Fair Lady*: 'Why can't a woman be more like a man?' or vice versa. How do your individual personalities complement and strengthen your partnership?

'A friend is one who knows us, but loves us anyway.' (Fr Jerome Cummings)

EPHESIANS 5:22, 25, 28, 33

Self-giving

*A wife should put her husband first, as she does the Lord...
A husband should love his wife as much as Christ loved the
church and gave his life for it... So each husband should
love his wife as much as he loves himself, and each wife
should respect her husband.*

True love puts others first. The marriage service places great emphasis on mutual respect and self-giving love.

How much do you love yourself? We instinctively shy away from pushing ourselves forward, while popular culture exhorts us to look after Number One, 'because you're worth it'. But here, Paul is encouraging husbands and wives to put the prosperity of the partnership first, ahead of their own success.

We may need to ask who will best be able to care for pre-school children, whose career can be put on hold, and what the priorities are for the home, at any given stage of the marriage. No one partner should give way every time. Today there is far greater flexibility in the way we organize our lives than there was for our parents.

Paul outlines principles that still hold true. Love puts the other first. Both should seek what is best for the marriage and for each other before themselves. Equally, there needs to be a right understanding of who we are before God. It's no good always deferring to our partner, without thinking through the issues together. God loves us unconditionally and totally, giving his Son for us. He wants us to have this same love for others, including those closest to us.

When is it most difficult to be selfless in deferring to each other, and why?

ACTS 4:32b, 34b–35

Selfless living

*None of them claimed that their possessions were their own,
and they shared everything they had with each other…
Everyone who owned land or houses would sell them and
bring the money to the apostles. Then they would give the
money to anyone who needed it.*

'All that I am I give to you, and all that I have I share with you.' This wedding promise encapsulates selfless living. Marriage offers the opportunity and challenge to live out these values on a daily basis, 'within the love of God', as the promise says.

The reality of such a commitment is hard. In our individualistic culture, where we are told we have a right to what we want, when we want it, such altruism is harder still. No surprise, then, if the vow is reinterpreted as 'All that you are, I demand of you, and all that I have, I retain the right to keep'! How do we avoid this? How do we learn to live selflessly in order to strengthen our marriages?

It takes practice. The longer we have been single, the harder it is to adjust to sharing our resources of possessions and money, time and energy. The jump from 'mine' and 'yours' to 'ours' is crucial, and the very words we use can either help or hinder the shift. As we grow together, we need to discuss what we both expect, to work out how much is 'enough' and what our financial priorities are.

Anna bumped into an old friend in the supermarket. Her husband has just retired, but his pension is worth far less than they had hoped and her dreams of retiring early have evaporated. They will sell their home and move. Yet there was no bitterness as she told her story. She and her husband are in it together, and will support each other through the changes that lie ahead.

What opportunities and challenges are there for you in the promise to give all and share all?

SONG OF SONGS 4:12, 15b; 8:6b–7

Sexual love (part 1)

My bride, my very own, you are a garden, a fountain closed off to all others… and a refreshing stream from Mount Lebanon… The passion of love bursting into flame is more powerful than death, stronger than the grave. Love cannot be drowned by oceans or floods; it cannot be bought, no matter what is offered.

Crowds jostle at the Chelsea Flower Show, anxious for the best view of the show gardens. Designs include tranquil water features, drifts of planting, leafy canopies, vivid colours and cool shades of green. Such features inspire the senses and touch us in ways that cannot easily be measured.

The writer of Song of Songs taps into the universal truth that gardens feed the soul. They are private places to be cherished and nurtured; they don't look after themselves. So it is with a loving relationship. Being in a garden heightens all five senses; being with the one we love quickens our perception of beauty.

The sexual relationship within each marriage is unique, as both partners seek to give refreshment, delight and satisfaction to each other. We need to be ready to give ourselves, rather than to make demands. As we learn to use the best 'languages of love' to communicate with each other, so we will become more relaxed and confident in our sexual partnership.

Sexual love is God's gift to humanity, and marriage is the relationship within which it is to be enjoyed, the walled garden that offers security and protection to those within. Sex is God's creation, his gift to bring us joy and fulfilment.

Marriage is a partnership where we are renewed daily. Time spent with each other is like lingering in a beautiful garden. To paraphrase a well-known advertising slogan, where will you go today to renew your love?

SONG OF SONGS 5:10–11, 14–16 (NRSV, ABRIDGED)

Sexual love (part 2)

My beloved is all radiant and ruddy, distinguished among ten thousand. His head is the finest gold; his locks are wavy, black as a raven… His arms are rounded gold, set with jewels. His body is ivory work, encrusted with sapphires. His legs are alabaster columns, set upon bases of gold… This is my beloved and this is my friend.

The bride in Song of Songs is as outspoken in her praise of her husband as he is in his praise of her. She finds him desirable, and tells him so. They are both lovers and friends. But what happens when raven-black locks turn grey, and the early passion fades? How much does sex still feature? Clearly there will be times in our marriages when we have less energy and opportunity to express our love sexually. Yet the communication of which sex is a vital part continues. We find new ways to express love, and we continue to share our lives, and ourselves, as much as we can.

Nick's grandmother was married three times in her 97 years. Her vivid memories of her first love, Cyril, never faded. Sixty years after his death he still held a special place in her heart, the husband of her youth. She went on to marry less happily in her 50s, and was widowed again. Some years later she met Arthur and was 'bowled over'. They were married for 18 years, through their 70s and 80s. They formed a strong, deep partnership. Both had known great love and loss in their first marriages, and both delighted in God's gift of love to them in their old age.

'Love is a temporary madness. It erupts like volcanoes and then subsides… Your mother and I had it, we had roots that grew toward each other underground, and when all the pretty blossom had fallen from our branches we found that we were one tree and not two.' (Louis de Bernieres)

MONDAY

PROVERBS 3:5–7

Plans and problems

With all your heart you must trust the Lord and not your own judgment. Always let him lead you, and he will clear the road for you to follow. Don't ever think that you are wise enough, but respect the Lord and stay away from evil.

We live in an age in which we believe that we can control everything about our lives. 'Don't you have a life-plan?' Nick was asked recently. Even if we do, there will be occasions when, due to circumstances beyond our control, we will have to trust God. In marriage, we choose our partner, or at least we like to think it was our choice! We reckon that we stand a good chance of 'making a go of it' together.

When things go wrong (and they may), it doesn't mean that we've made bad choices or that God is not on our side any more. On the contrary, God corrects everyone he loves. Shared setbacks, both small and significant, can enable a couple to find new depths in their relationship.

Sometimes God offers us his direction out of love. At other times he is happy for us to choose. It delights him to see us stepping out positively, as a parent is thrilled to see children make wholesome life choices for themselves. As the story of your marriage unfolds, take time together to look back and recognize God's guidance along the way. It will help you to keep going when problems arise.

We took a canal holiday with friends. On the last day, we had to negotiate a mile-long tunnel. Dark and dank, it seemed to last for ever, with only a pinprick of light ahead. The experience of steering our boat over the previous days, however, enabled us to keep going forward with confidence, however little we could see at the time.

'Trust the Lord and his mighty power. Remember his miracles and all his wonders and his fair decisions.' (Psalm 105:4–5)

PHILIPPIANS 3:12–13, 15 (ABRIDGED)

Keep going!

I have not yet reached my goal, and I am not perfect. But Christ has taken hold of me. So I keep on running and struggling to take hold of the prize… But I forget what is behind, and I struggle for what is ahead… All of us who are mature should think in this same way.

'Never, never give up.' Thus responded an American football coach, when asked the secret of his team's success. Whatever the score, each member knew he could rely on the others to be there for him.

When we marry, we agree that there is no adverse circumstance that will drive us to give up on the marriage, because of the unshakeable resolve that each possesses to 'keep on keeping on'. Nothing will come between our love for each other. So why do so many couples divorce? Sadly, when problems arise, if one partner lacks determination to keep going, divorce can seem unavoidable. If both want to persevere, the marriage will nearly always survive.

Our daughter is a sprinter. Twice a week, sometimes more often, she trains hard, improving her fitness and technique. Even with talent, she knows that she will only win races if she works hard. In marriage, the same principle applies. We may be 'made for each other', but it is hard work maintaining, let alone improving our relationship. The goal of a marriage that is 'life-giving and life-long' makes it worthwhile spending time struggling, keeping going.

Sprinters are often advised not to look either side to see how fellow competitors are doing. We are to keep our eyes on the finishing tape and on Jesus, the starter and final judge. He also awards the prize!

'Christ in our beginning, Christ there at our end,
Christ be in our journey, Christ everlasting friend.' (David Adam)

PSALM 34:8 (NIV)

Taste and see!

Taste and see that the Lord is good;
blessed are those who takes refuge in him.

Following Jesus means that what we thought predictable is turned on its head. In the one biblical account of Jesus at a wedding, he amazes the guests by producing best wine from ordinary water (John 2:1–10). Invite Jesus into your marriage and you run the (calculated, exciting) risk that even everyday life will be transformed.

God delights to renew us and our marriage. As we face new situations together, we will be surprised by what we learn. The birth of our first child was one such occasion for us: an opportunity to be amazed by each other's endurance and determination, as Anna made it through labour and Nick didn't go away. Dare to surprise your partner now and then with 'best wine' when they least expect it! Even a cup of tea will do occasionally.

Jesus came that we might have life in all its fullness (John 10:10), not to keep us stuck in a rut of predictability. How stultifying to end up in a *Groundhog Day* marriage, frustrating and monotonous! One of the underlying messages of that film is that we need to put others first in order to love and be loved ourselves. How true of Christian marriage, where we put each other's needs first.

Men and women really are made in God's image, as shown most clearly when we love each other. It is not just human love, but God's love that we experience: the powerful, transforming love of God himself. That is why people grow and mature in exciting new ways within a loving marriage relationship.

'Christian experience is not so much a matter of imitating a leader as accepting and receiving a new quality of life, a life infinitely more profound and dynamic and meaningful than human life without Christ.' (H.A. Williams)

LUKE 6:37–38 (ABRIDGED)

Forgiveness

*Jesus said: 'Don't judge others, and God won't judge you.
Don't be hard on others, and God won't be hard on you.
Forgive others, and God will forgive you. If you give to others,
you will be given a full amount in return… The way you
treat others is the way you will be treated.'*

Jesus often talked about forgiveness: 'Do as you would be done
by.' We can resolve to follow this rule, but it becomes hardest to
do when we most need to do it. When it is someone we love
who lets us down, the sense of betrayal is acute. Thankfully, Jesus
understands this fully, and yet his cry from the cross demonstrates
the releasing power of God's forgiveness: 'Father, forgive these
people! They don't know what they're doing' (Luke 23:34).

Forgiving others is the condition by which we are able to receive
God's forgiveness. Unless we forgive others, we will not be forgiven,
because our hearts will be closed to the grace and mercy of God.

Within the privileged position of a marriage, it can be easy to
nit-pick and point out each other's faults, to be harsh with each
other, to criticize rather than to compliment. Get into the habit of
seeing the positive. Decide to build up each other's self-esteem
rather than undermining it. Jesus implies that we are to look at
ourselves through God's eyes. Measure yourself and your partner
by Jesus himself, who recognized us as needing forgiveness and
was prepared to give his life so that we could receive it.

That is the challenge of these verses for both marriage partners,
and the reward is promised. Forgive and you will be forgiven. It
would be a risky policy, except that God always keeps his promises.

*Anticipate those times when you will find forgiveness hardest. Share
them now with your partner, so that you'll both recognize the times when
you need God to help you forgive.*

PROVERBS 5:15–18 (NRSV)

Loyalty and faithfulness

Drink water from your own cistern, flowing water from your own well. Should your springs be scattered abroad, streams of water in the streets? Let them be for yourself alone, and not for sharing with strangers. Let your fountain be blessed, and rejoice in the wife of your youth.

The watery image may make us think of garden makeovers, but these verses are really about the shame and damage that adultery causes. God asks us to remain loyal to one another and to him, whatever challenging situations we are facing.

The temptation to look elsewhere is all around us. Our perception, fuelled by the media, may be that virtues such as loyalty and faithfulness are no longer so important, but they can still make an impact. At a 20-year anniversary school reunion, Nick was in conversation with a dozen contemporaries. Each in turn listed the number of marriages and relationships they had had since leaving school. He realized that he would be the last to speak but, contrary to expectations, found that they were all amazed and impressed when he explained that he had been married to the same wife for over 20 years. 'Wow! What's the secret?' came the response. He could have quoted these verses.

At a young couple's wedding, the bride's grandfather, who had been married in the same church 60 years previously, gave one of the readings. His presence, with his wife, reminded us of the far-reaching blessing of a faithful marriage, for the wider community.

As we 'drink from our own fountain' and nurture what we have, our marriage will be blessed. If we put our energies into building up what we are given, we in turn will be blessed. We'll be content.

'Let their love for each other be a seal upon their hearts, and a crown upon their heads.' (Common Worship *Marriage Service*)

LUKE 24:13–16, 28–31 (ABRIDGED)

Walking with Jesus

That same day two of Jesus' disciples were going to the village of Emmaus… As they were talking and thinking about what had happened, Jesus came near and started walking along beside them. But they did not know who he was… When the two of them came near the village… they begged him, 'Stay with us! …' After Jesus sat down to eat, he took some bread. He blessed it and broke it. Then he gave it to them. At once they knew who he was, but he disappeared.

Closeness to Jesus makes for a fulfilled married relationship, even when, as on the Emmaus road, he is not recognized. So it might be for us. When we walk a lonely or difficult path, Jesus is with us. Only looking back do we see his footsteps alongside ours. He will reveal himself to us when we are ready to see him, and then his presence will quicken our hearts and keep us conversing with him.

The couple begged their mystery companion to stay with them. So might we, in our darkest hours, pray that God would 'stay with us' through the night, revealing his love and peace in the morning. As Jesus did for the couple on the road, he shares our sorrow and our joy. He asks questions of us, which enable us to know him better: 'What are you discussing?' He listens and responds.

Our first reading recounted how Adam and Eve forfeited the tree of life and broke their relationships with God and each other, hiding in their shame. Here, in a healing moment, those relationships are restored as Jesus, the bread of life, shares his very self with the travellers and their eyes are opened to see him.

'May your blessing come in full upon us. May we know your presence in our joys and in our sorrows. May we reach old age in the company of friends and come at last to your eternal kingdom, through Jesus Christ our Lord.' (Common Worship *Marriage Service*)

Bible reading notes from BRF

If you have found this booklet helpful and would like to continue reading the Bible regularly, you may like to explore BRF's three series of Bible reading notes.

NEW DAYLIGHT

New Daylight offers a devotional approach to reading the Bible. Each issue covers four months of daily Bible readings and reflection from a regular team of contributors, who represent a stimulating mix of church backgrounds. Each day's reading provides a Bible passage (text included), comment and prayer or thought for reflection. In *New Daylight* the Sundays and special festivals from the church calendar are noted on the relevant days, to help you appreciate the riches of the Christian year.

DAY BY DAY WITH GOD

Day by Day with God (published jointly with Christina Press) is written especially for women, with a regular team of contributors. Each four-monthly issue offers daily Bible readings, with key verses printed out, helpful comment, a prayer or reflection for the day ahead, and suggestions for further reading.

GUIDELINES

Guidelines is a unique Bible reading resource that offers four months of in-depth study written by leading scholars. Contributors are drawn from around the world, as well as the UK, and they represent a thought-provoking breadth of Christian tradition. *Guidelines* is written in weekly units consisting of six sections plus an introduction and a final section of points for thought and prayer.

If you would like to subscribe to one or more of these sets of Bible reading notes, please use the order form overleaf.

SUBSCRIPTIONS

❏ I would like to give a gift subscription (please complete both name and address sections below)

❏ I would like to take out a subscription myself (complete name and address details only once)

This completed coupon should be sent with appropriate payment to BRF. Alternatively, please write to us quoting your name, address, the subscription you would like for either yourself or a friend (with their name and address), the start date and credit card number, expiry date and signature if paying by credit card.

Gift subscription name _____

Gift subscription address_____

_____Postcode _____

Please send beginning with the January / May / September issue: (delete as applicable)

(please tick box)	UK	SURFACE	AIR MAIL
NEW DAYLIGHT	❏ £11.70	❏ £13.05	❏ £15.30
GUIDELINES	❏ £11.70	❏ £13.05	❏ £15.30
DAY BY DAY WITH GOD	❏ £12.45	❏ £13.80	❏ £16.05

Please complete the payment details below and send your coupon, with appropriate payment to: **BRF, First Floor, Elsfield Hall, 15–17 Elsfield Way, Oxford OX2 8FG.**

Your name _____

Your address _____

_____Postcode _____

Total enclosed £ _____ (cheques made payable to 'BRF')

Payment: cheque ❏ postal order ❏ Visa ❏ Mastercard ❏ Switch ❏

Card number: ⬚⬚⬚⬚⬚⬚⬚⬚⬚⬚⬚⬚⬚⬚⬚⬚⬚⬚⬚⬚

Expiry date of card: ⬚⬚⬚⬚   Issue number (Switch): ⬚⬚⬚⬚

Signature (essential if paying by credit/Switch card)

❏ Please do not send me further information about BRF publications.

BRF resources are available from your local Christian bookshop. BRF is a Registered Charity